Copyright © 2015 P. Blake

All Rights Reserved Worldwide

# BATHROOM RUSH!
## Coloring Book

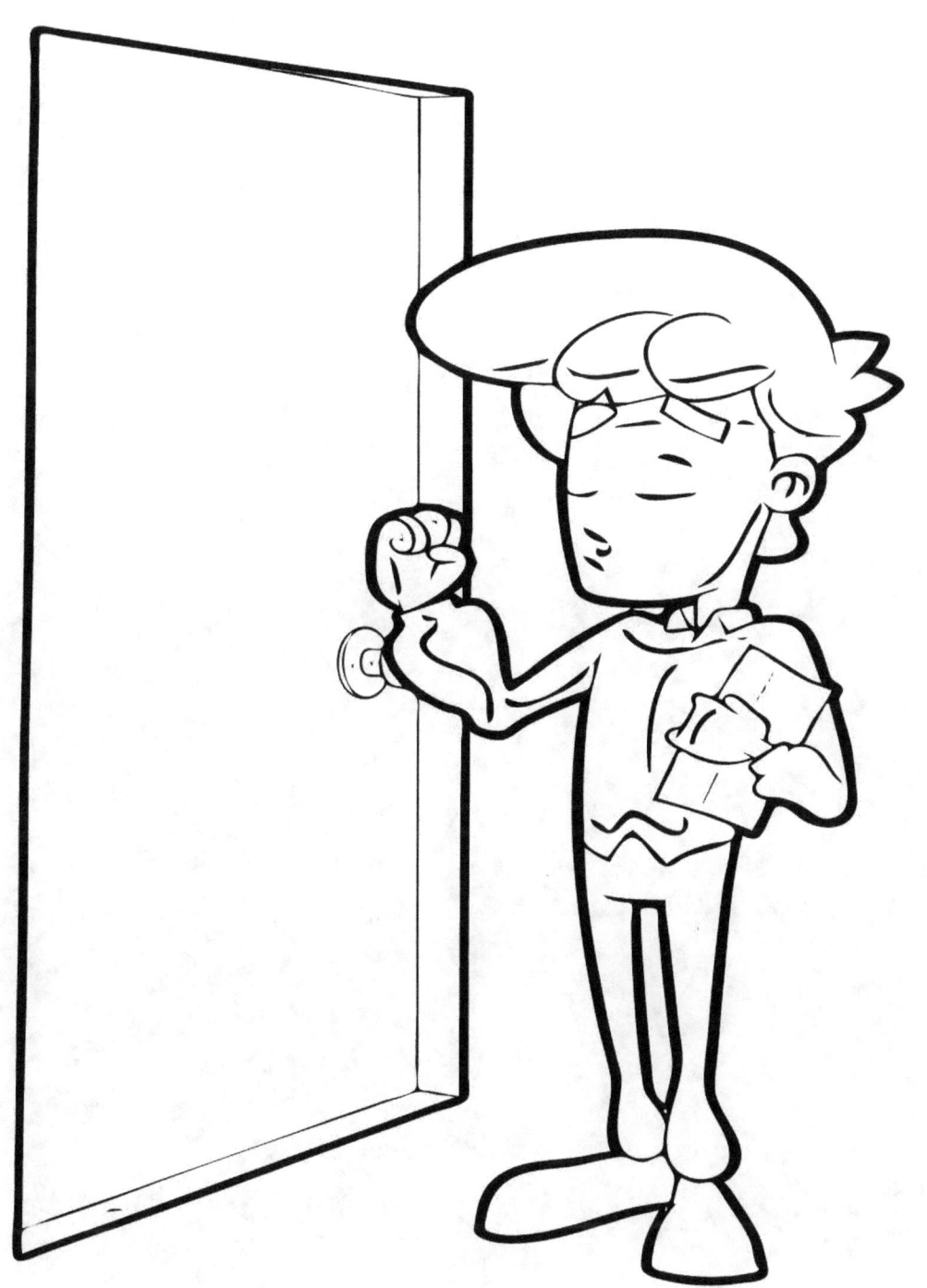

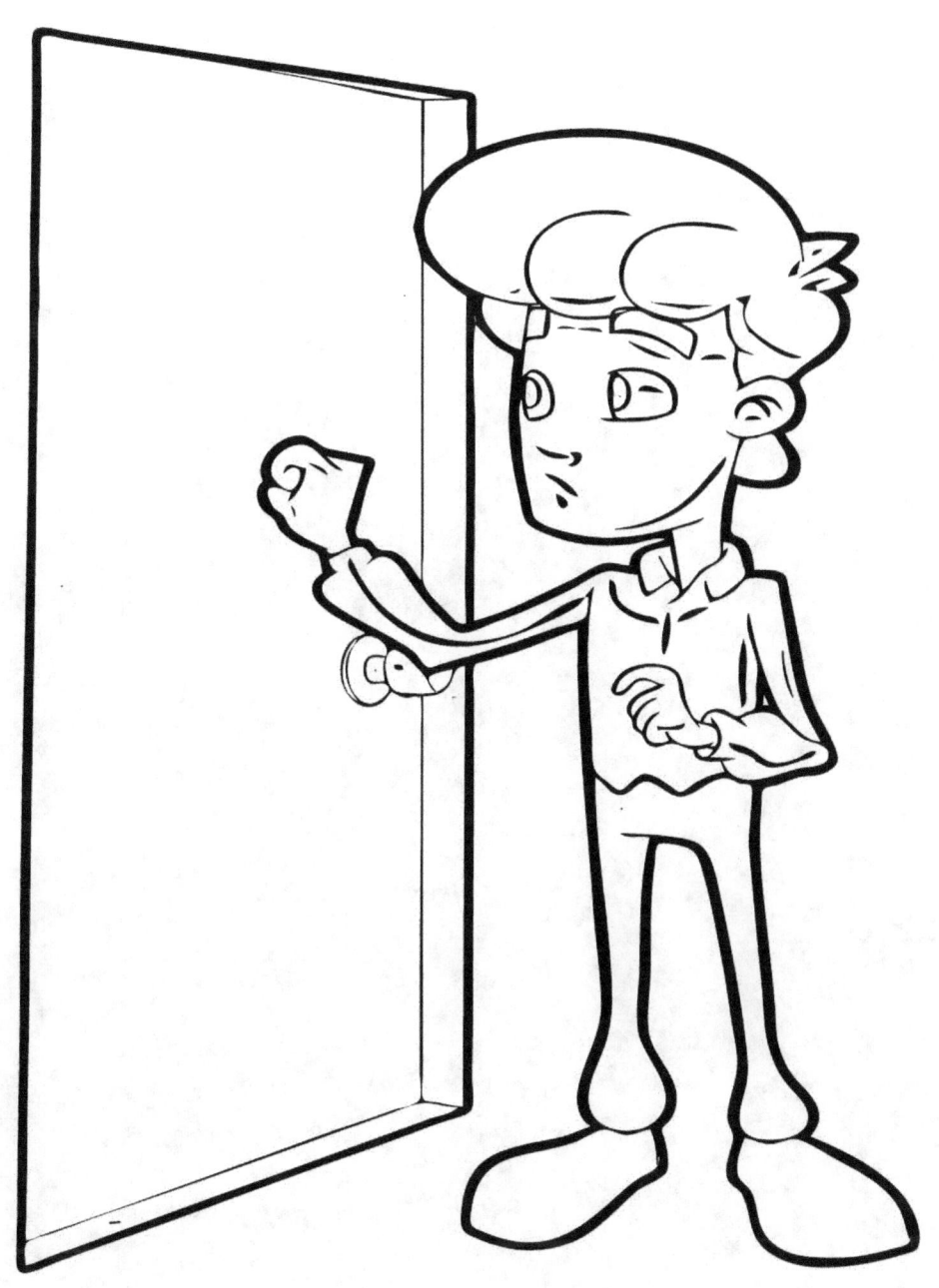

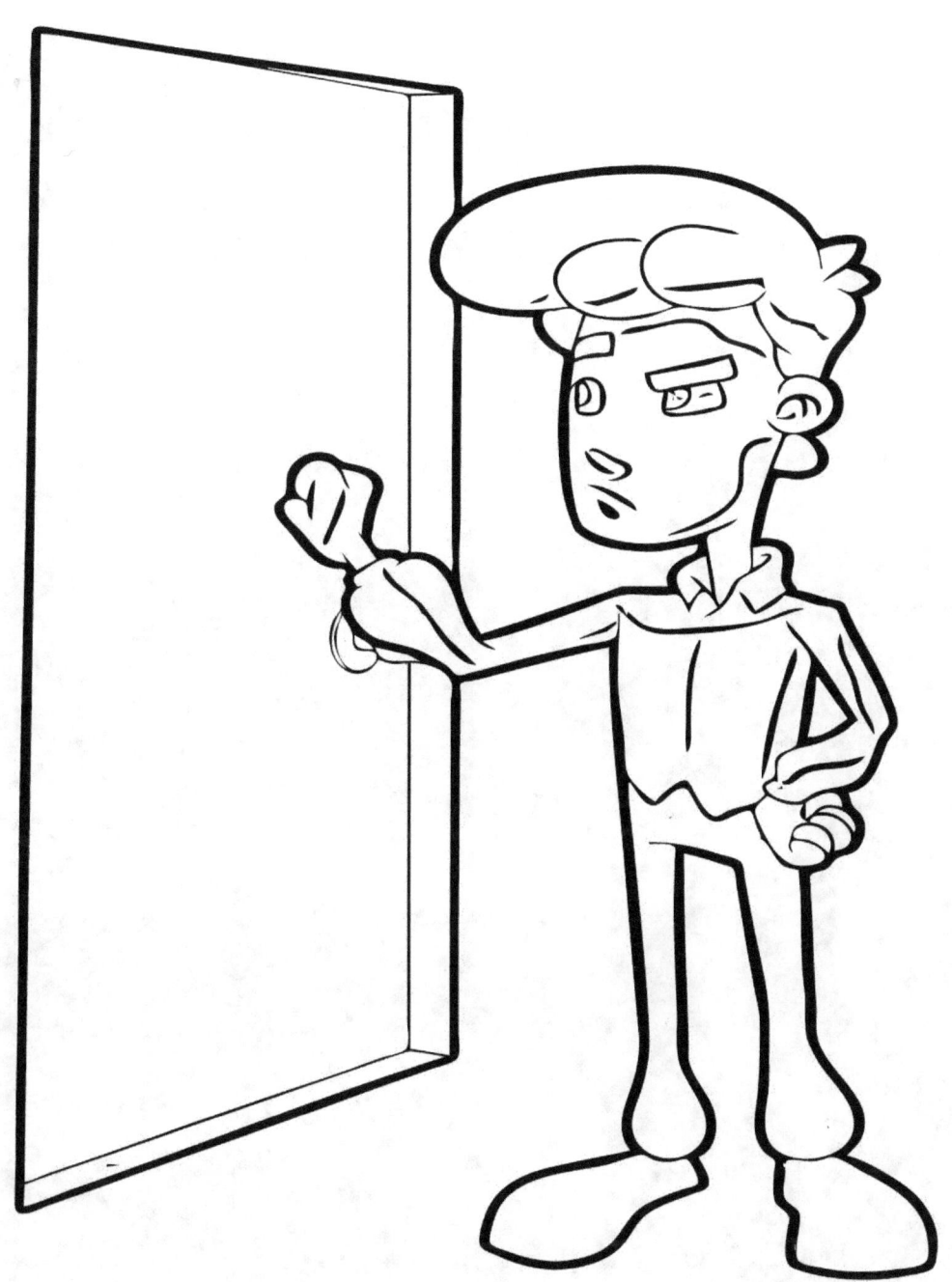

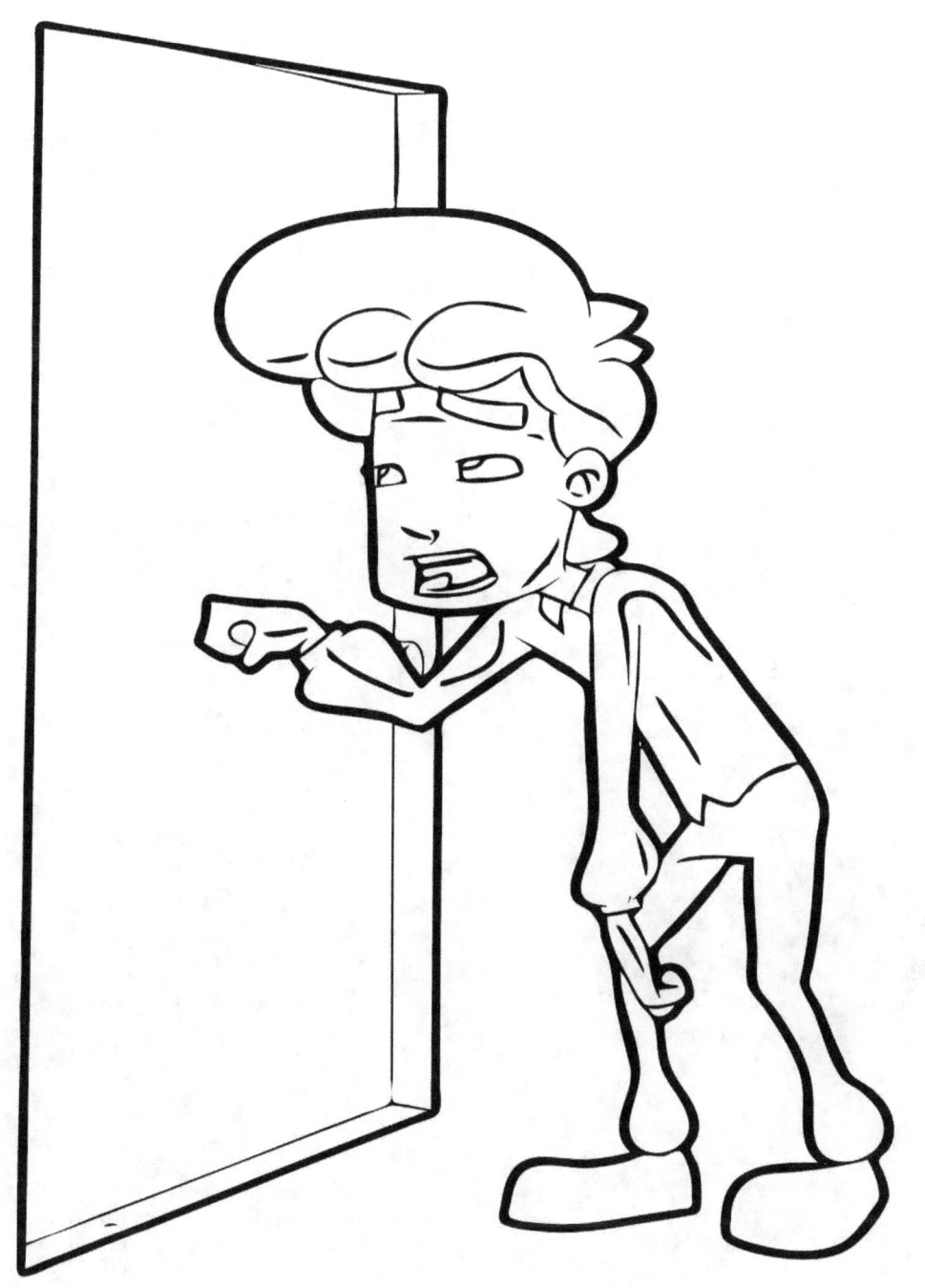

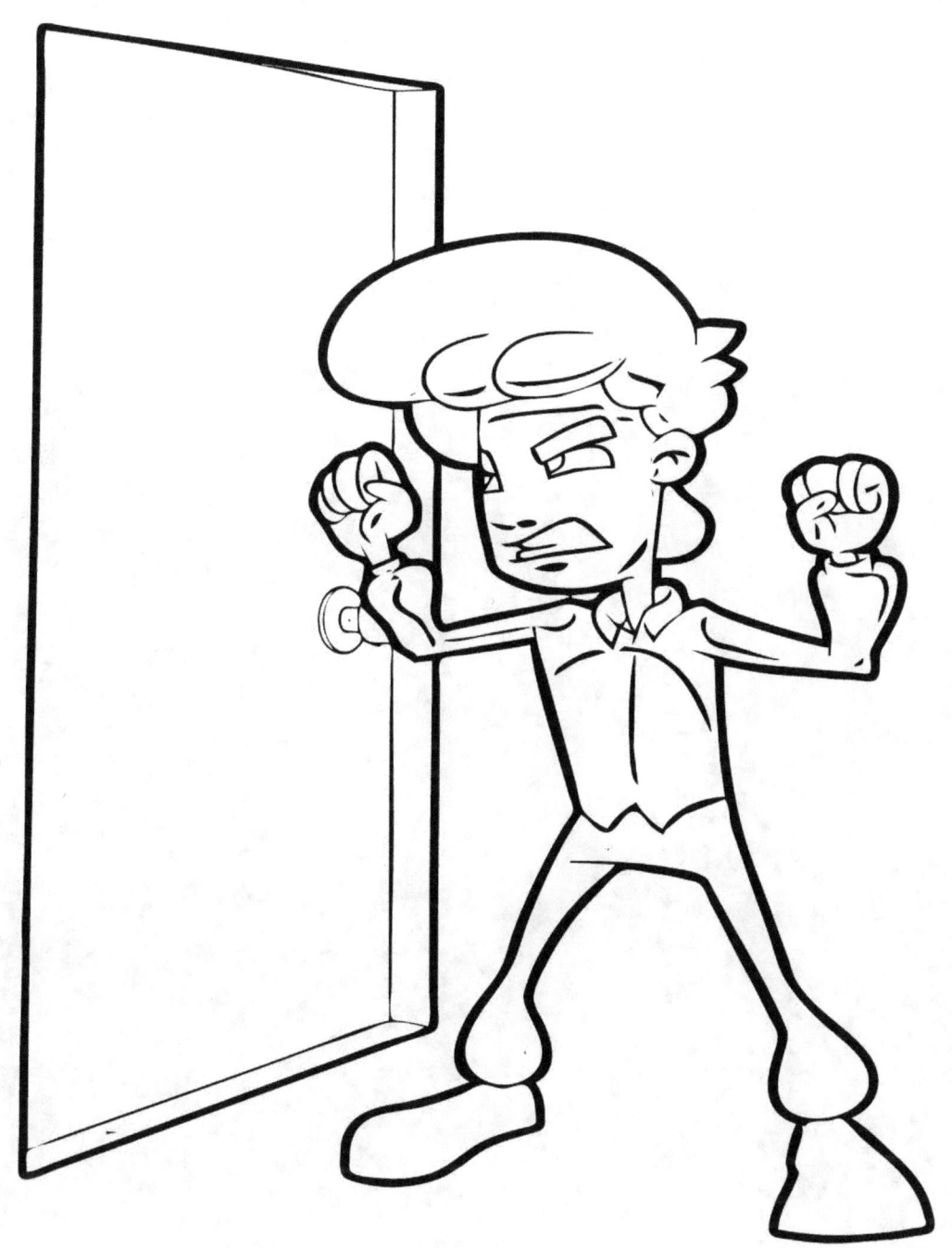

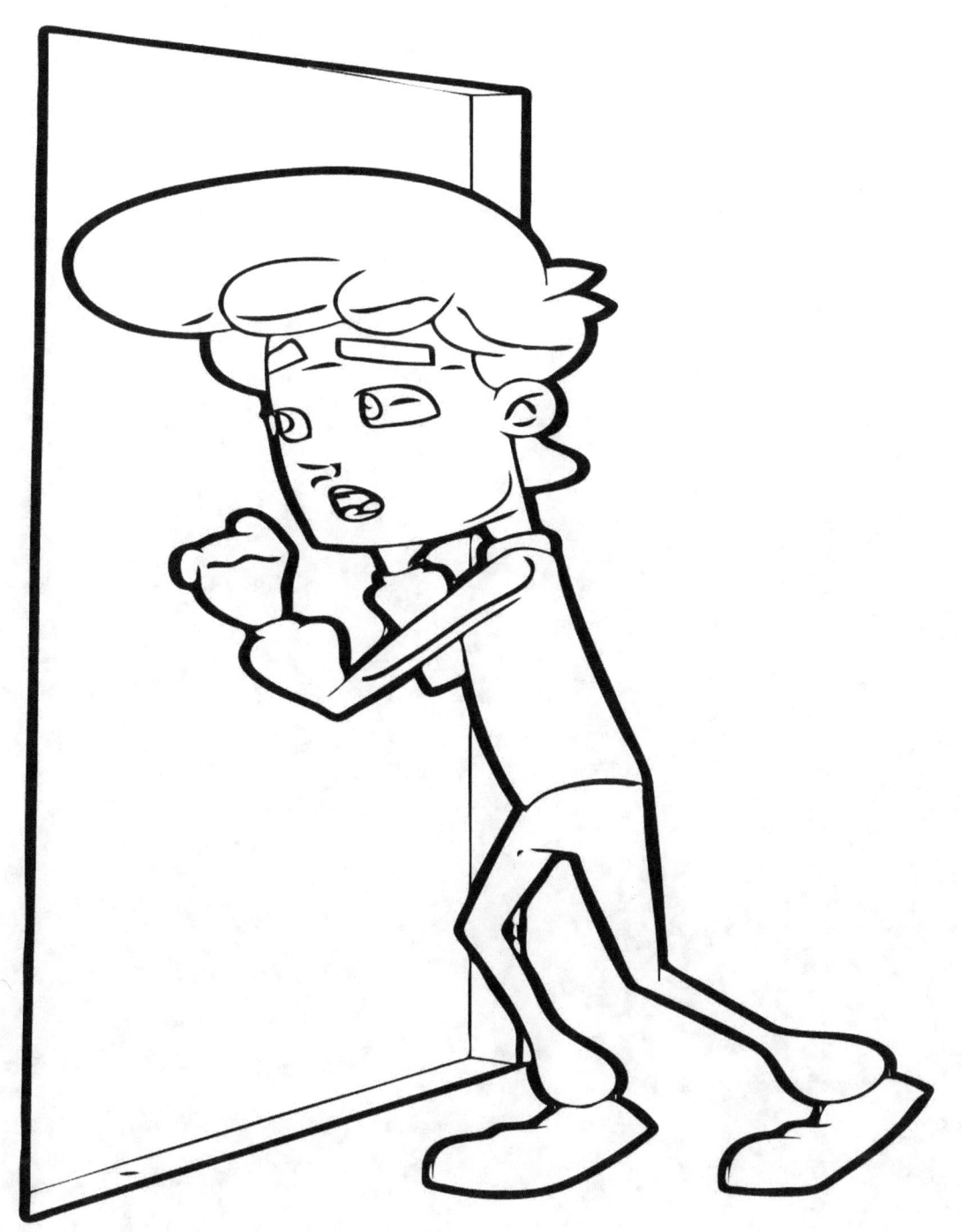

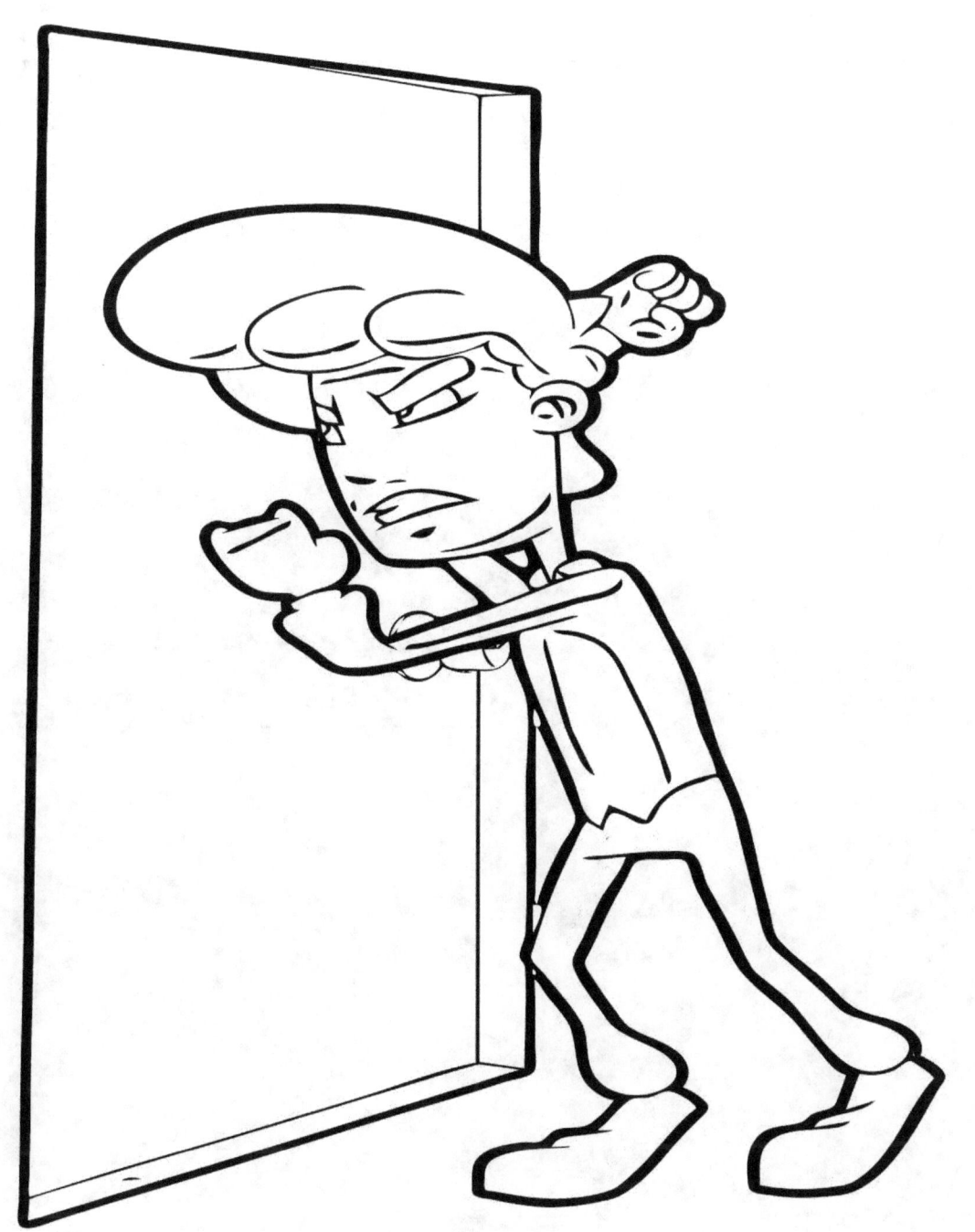

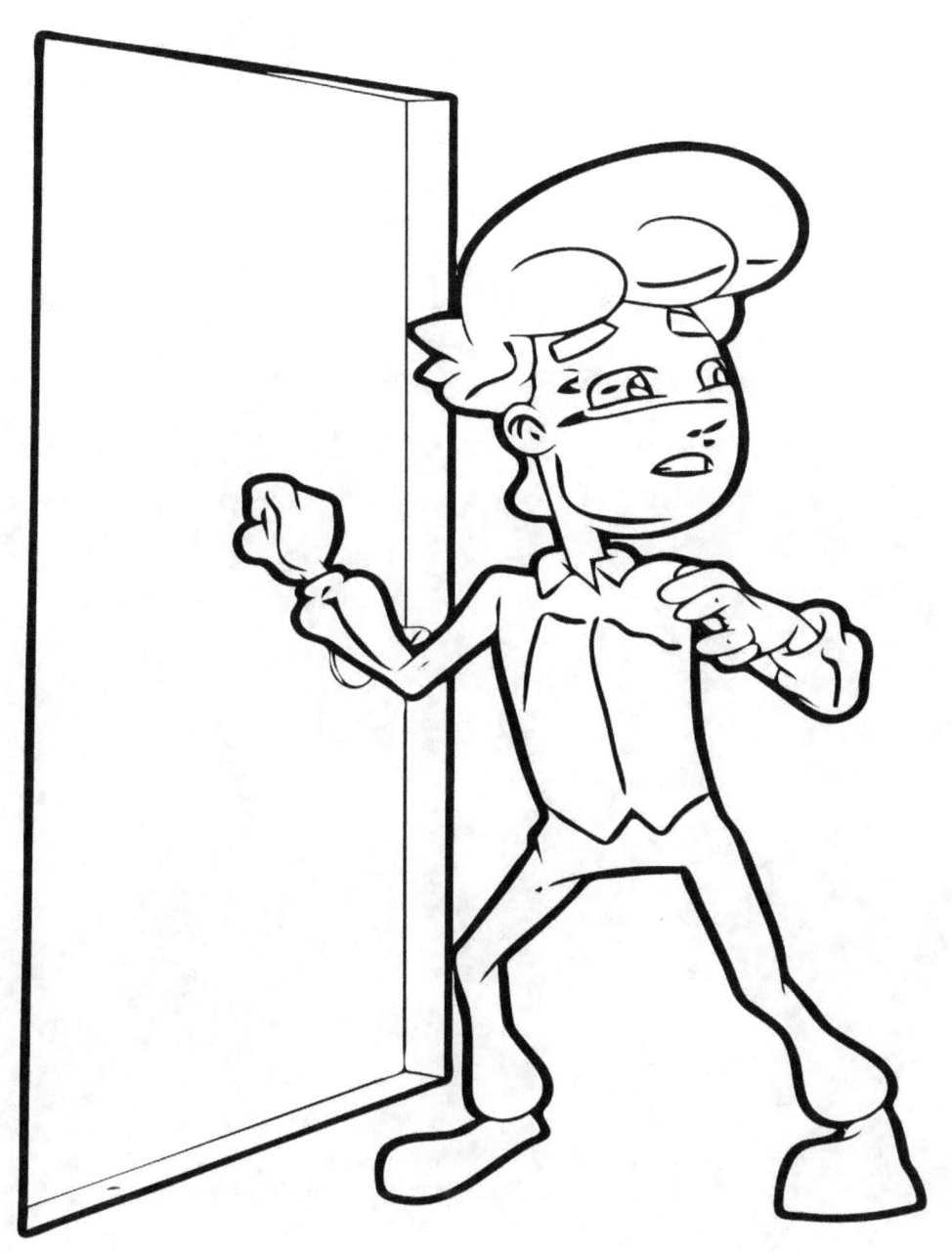

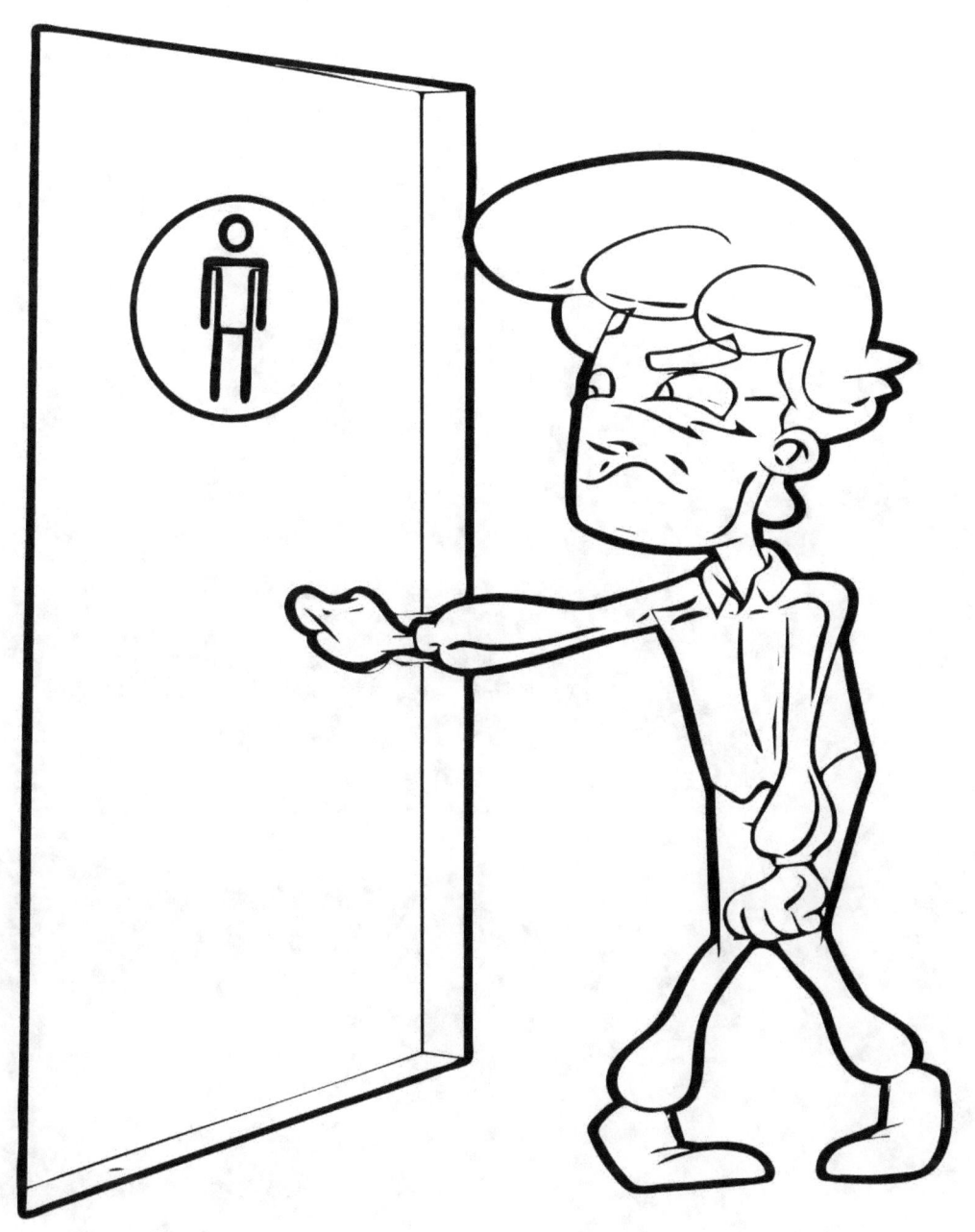

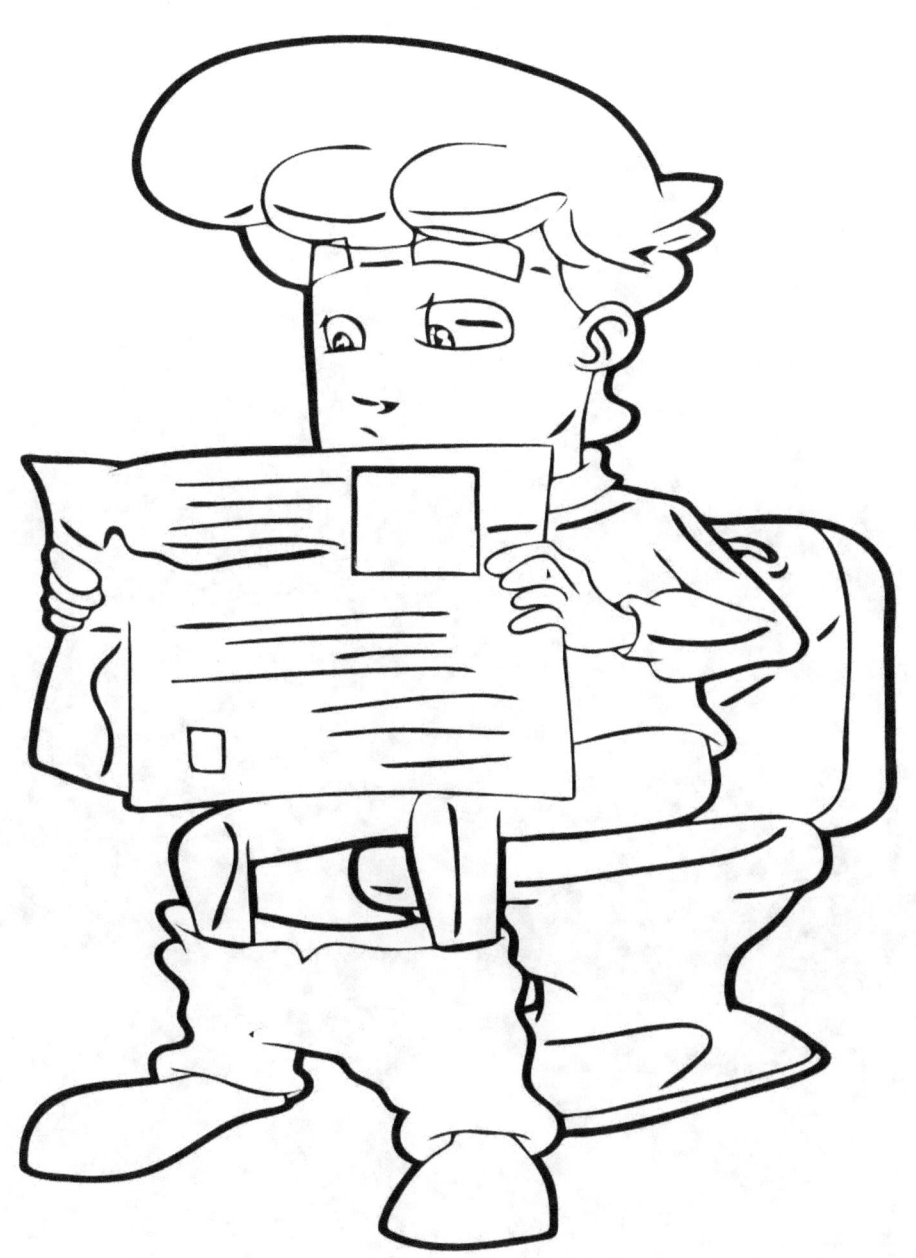

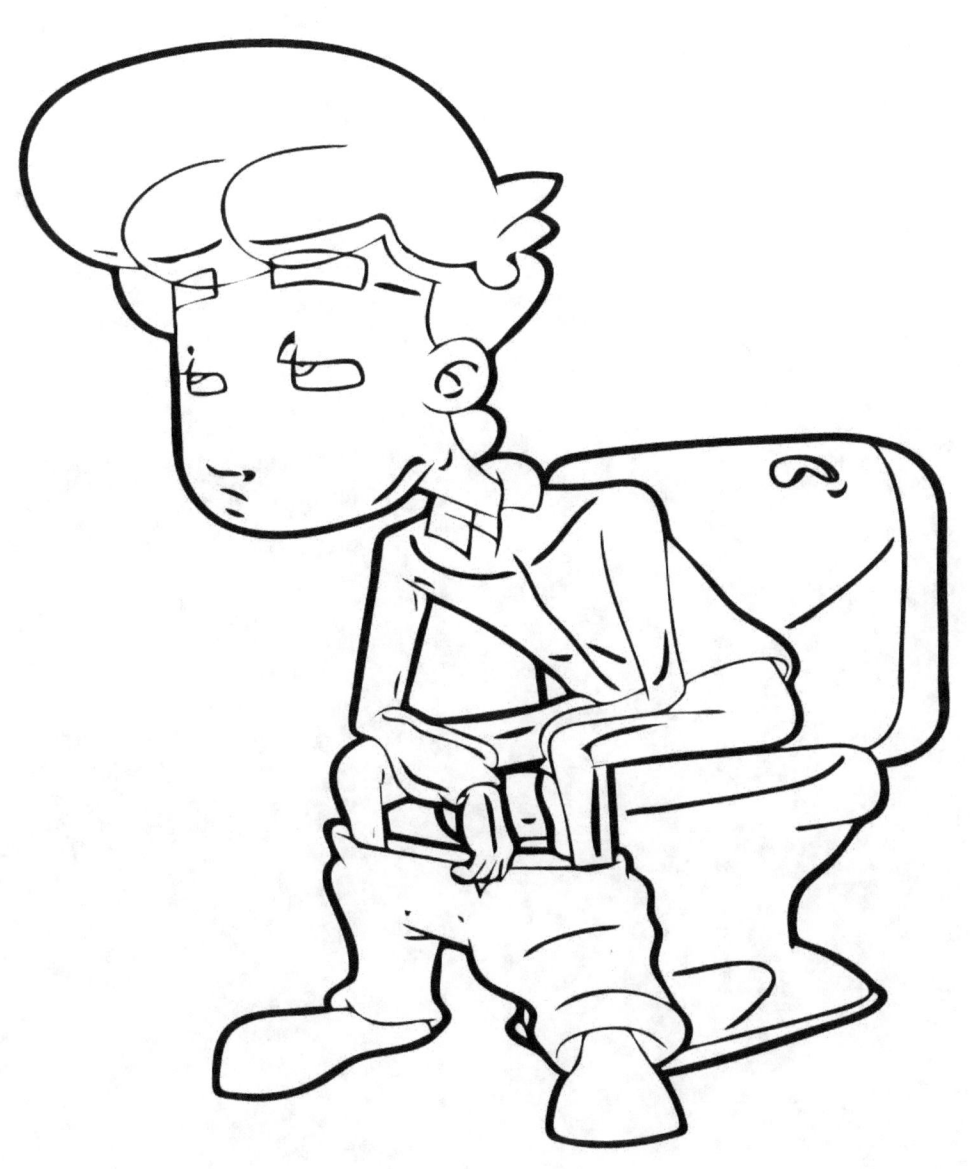

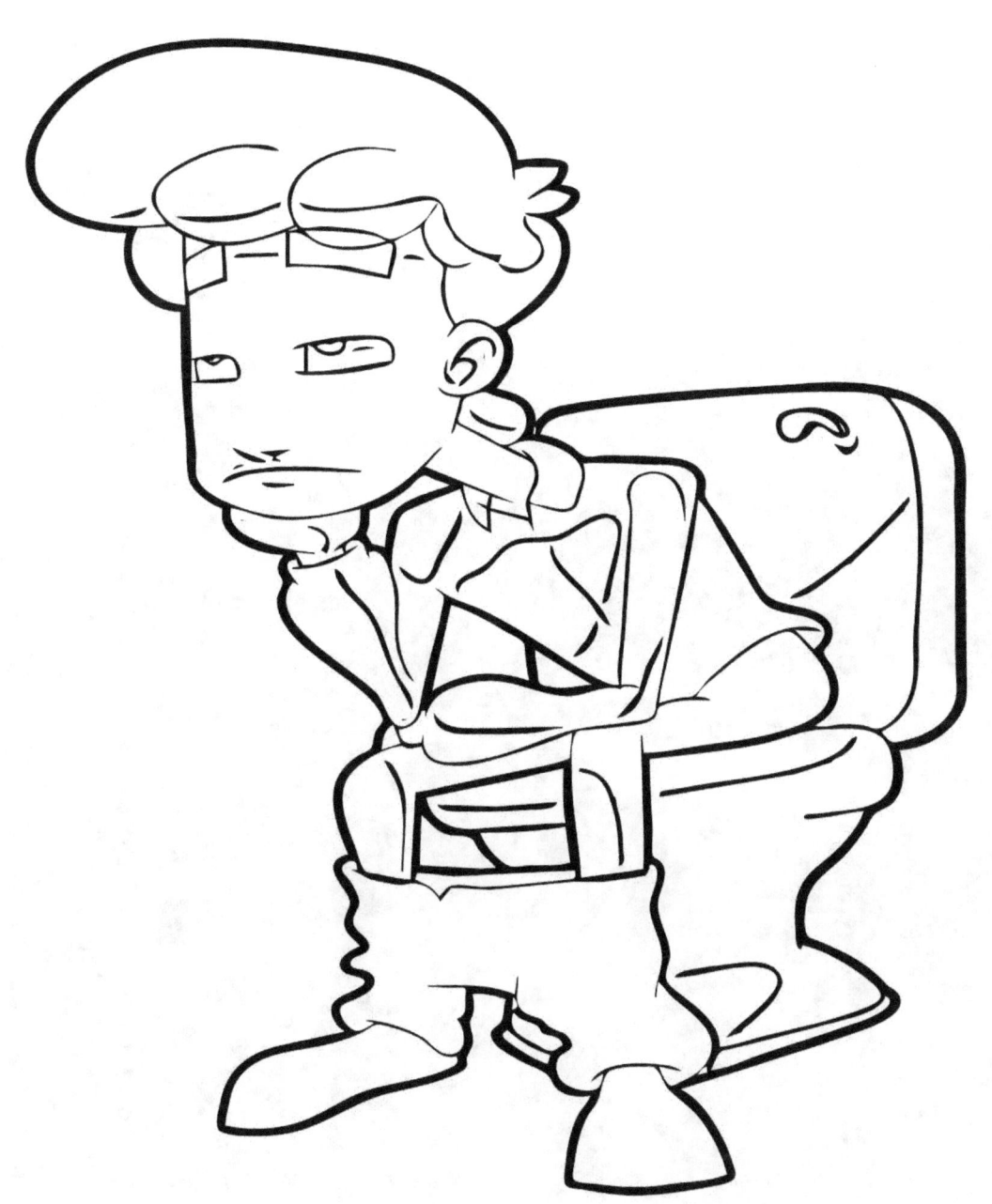

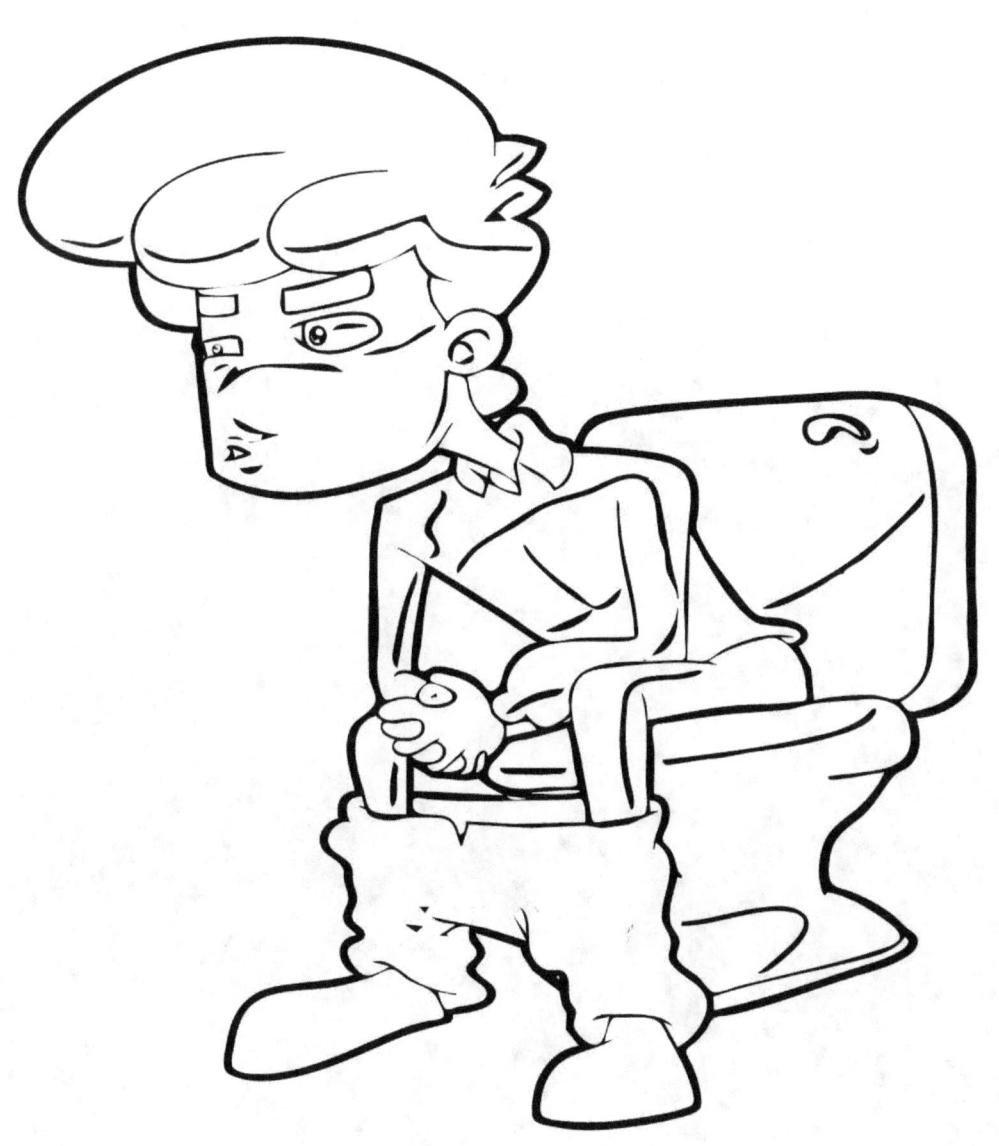

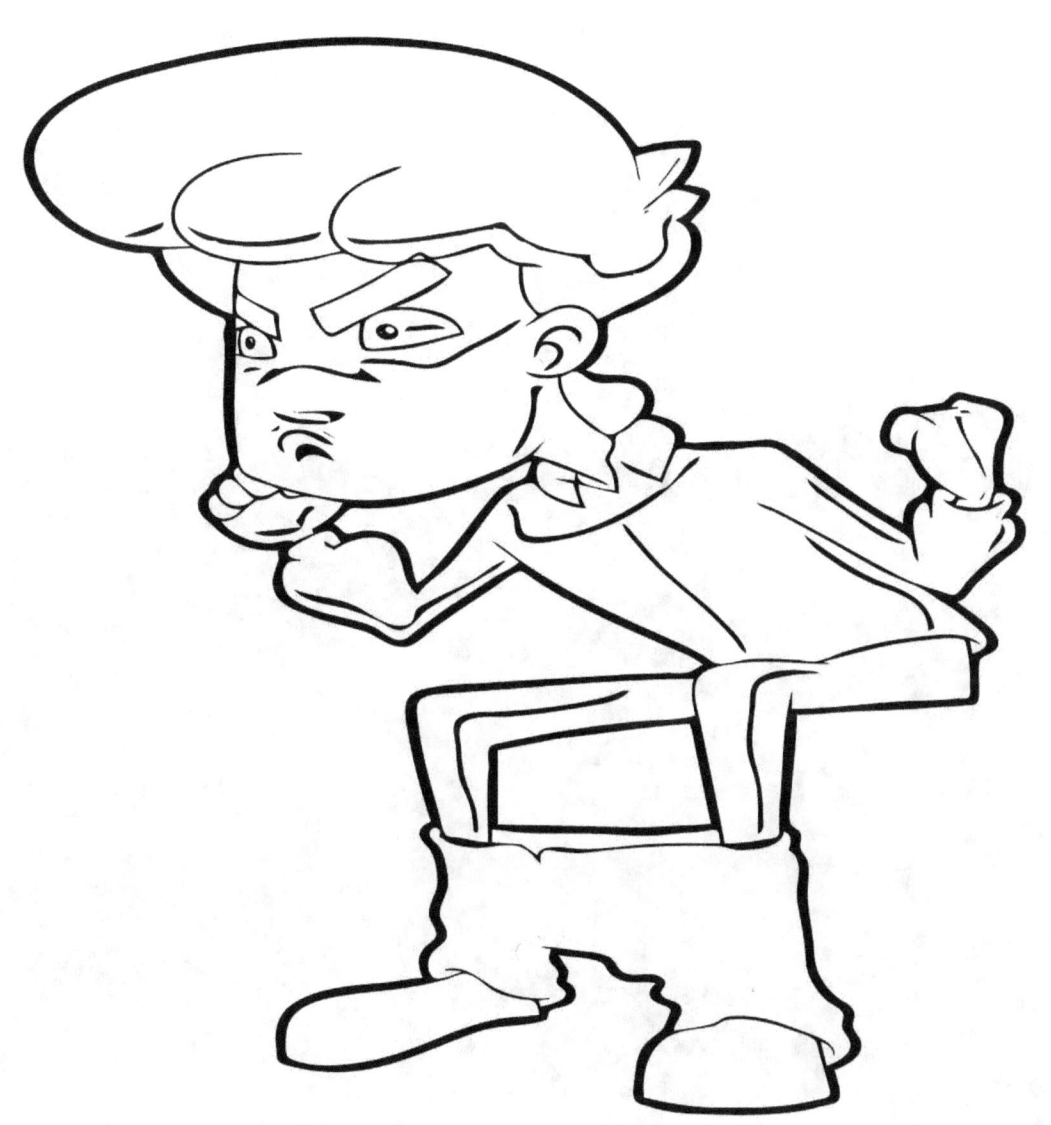

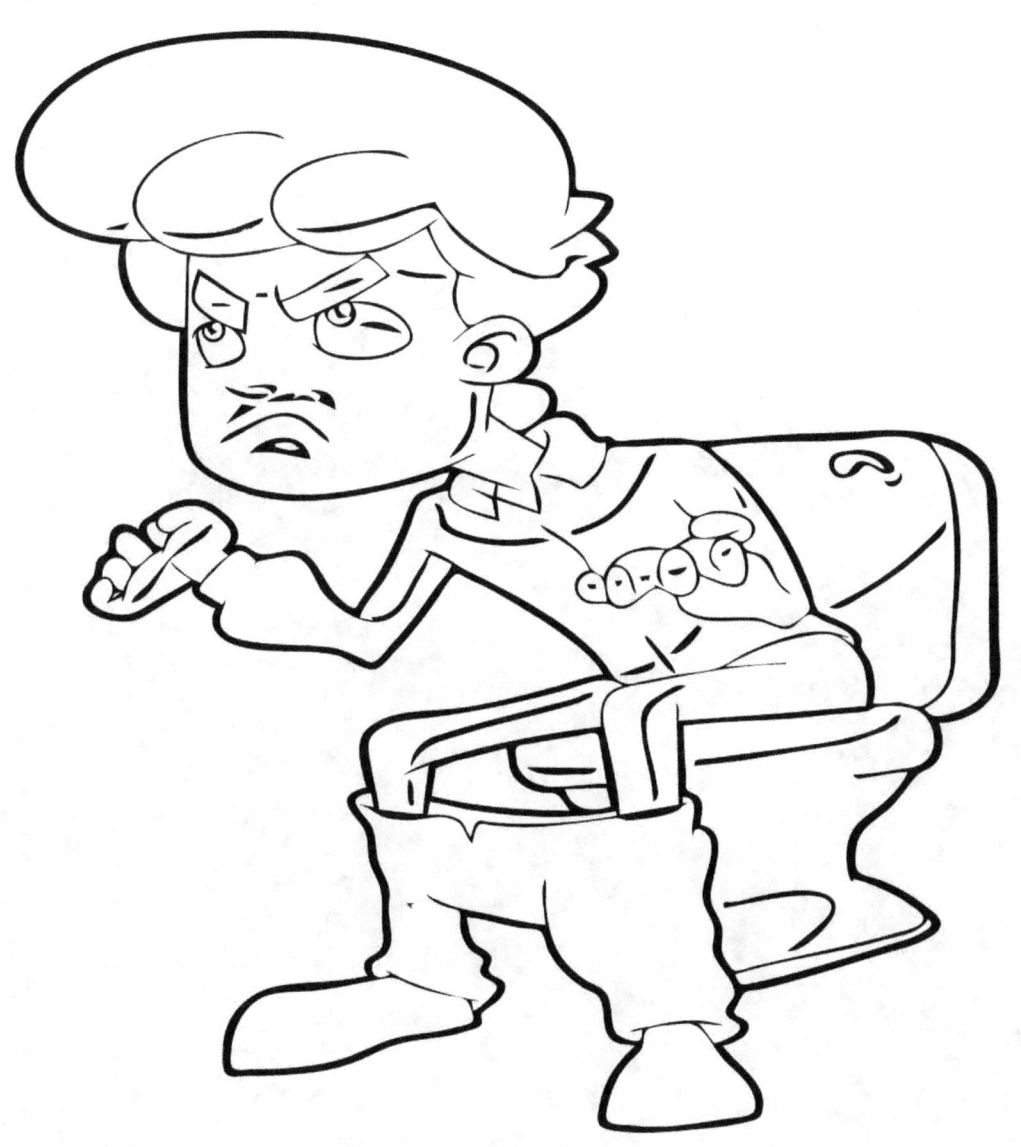

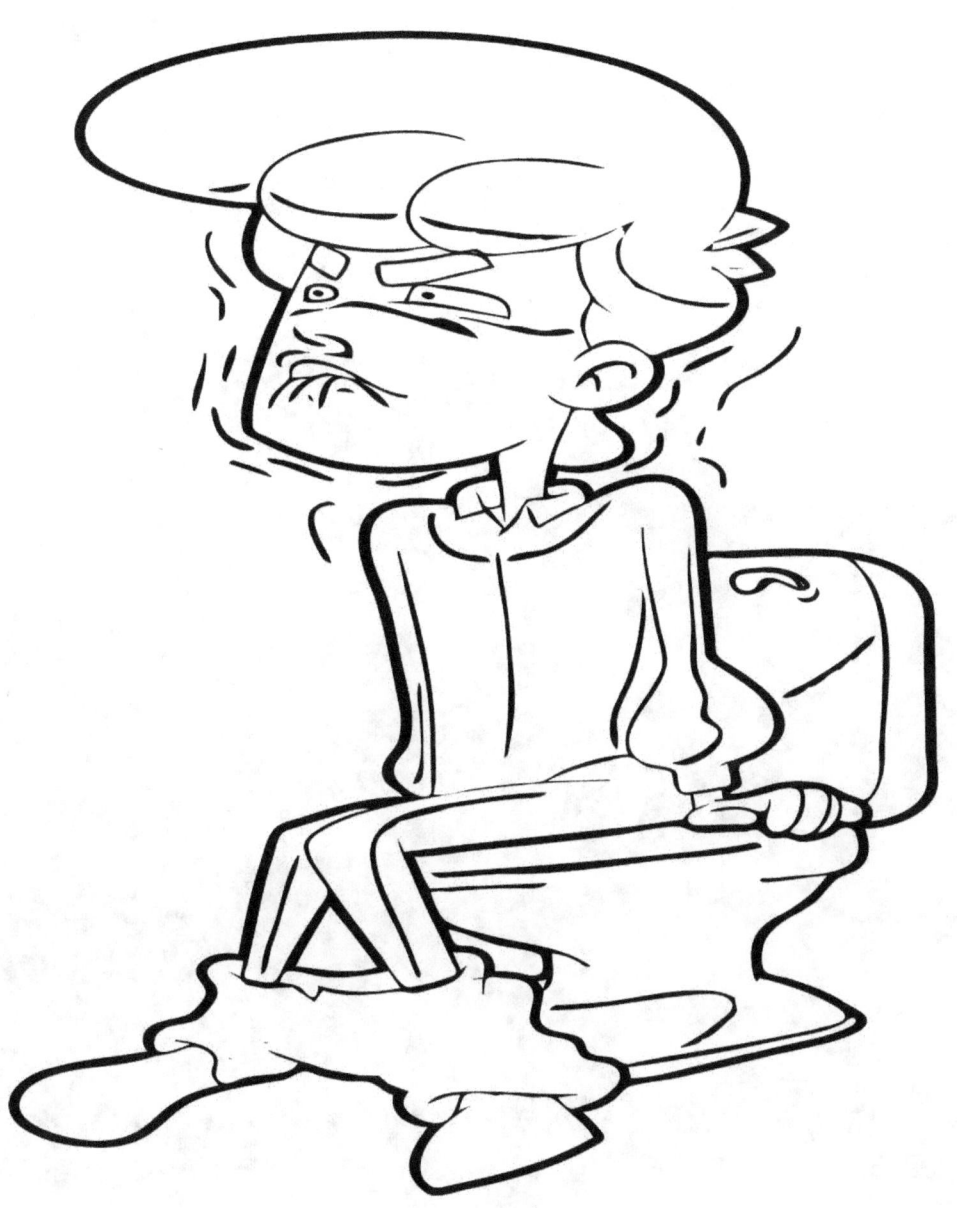

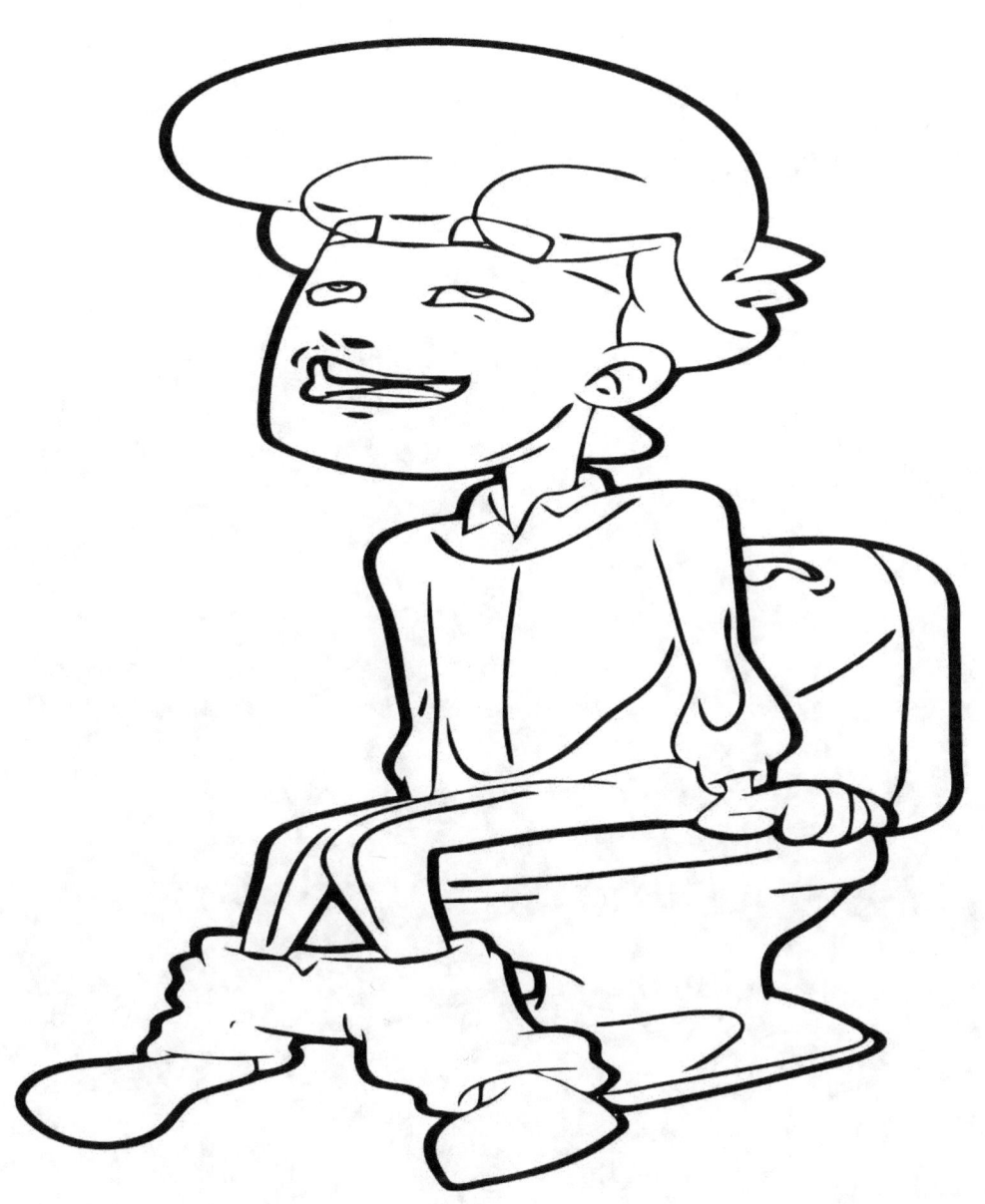

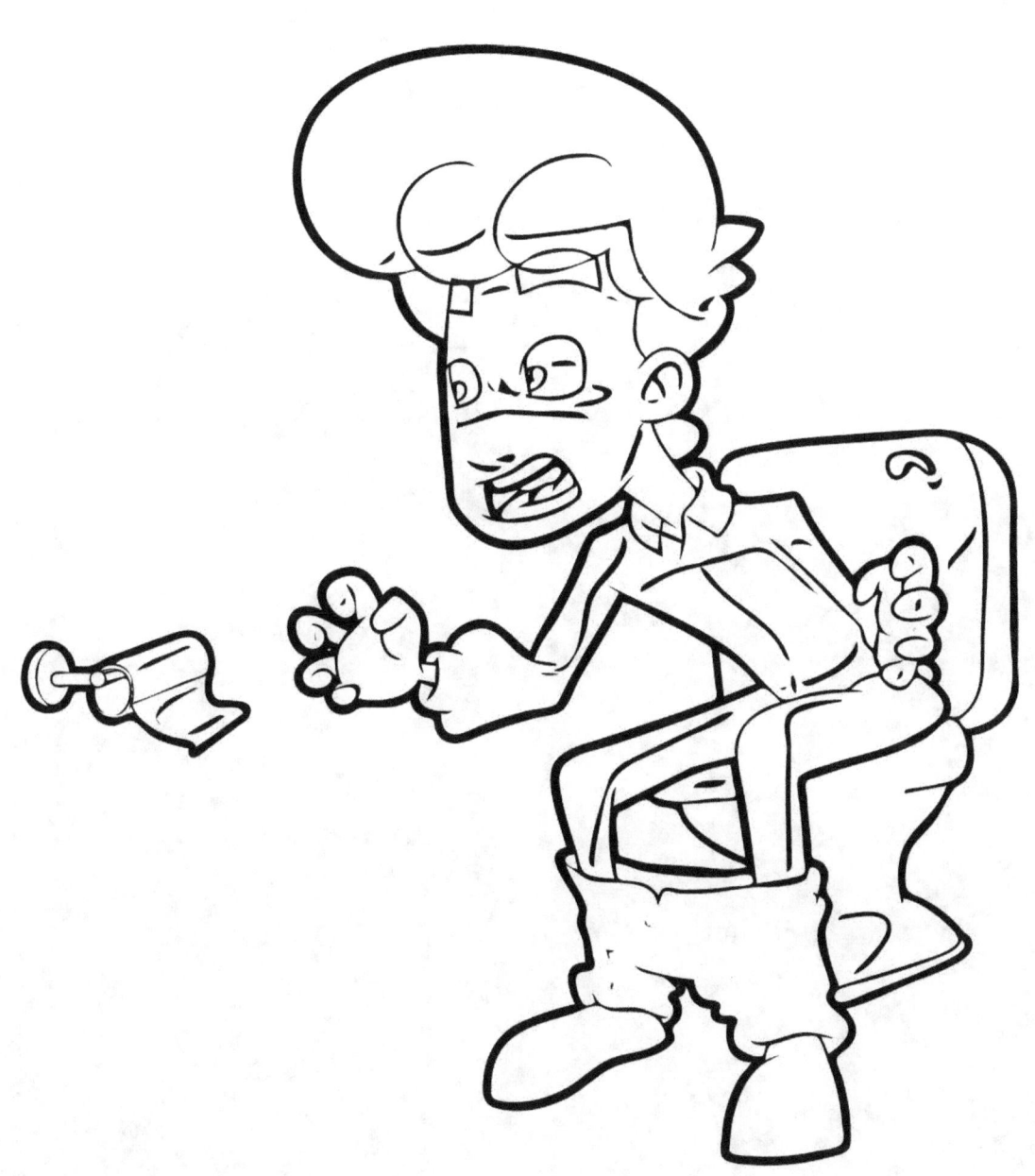

www.ingramcontent.com/pod-product-compliance
Lightning Source LLC
Chambersburg PA
CBHW081406170526
45166CB00010B/3226